The Appendix

Published by 404 Ink Limited
www.404Ink.com
@404Ink

Please note: Some references include URLs which may change or be unavailable
after publication of this book. All references within endnotes were accessible
and accurate as of July 2021 but may experience link rot from there on in.

Editing: Heather McDaid & Laura Jones
Typesetting: Laura Jones
Cover design: Luke Bird
Co-founders and publishers of 404 Ink: Heather McDaid & Laura Jones

Print ISBN: 978-1-912489-40-4
Ebook ISBN: 978-1-912489-41-1

Printed and bound in Great Britain by Clays Ltd, Elcograf S.p.A.

404 Ink acknowledges support for this title from
Creative Scotland via the Crowdmatch initiative.

LOTTERY FUNDED

The Appendix

Transmasculine Joy
in a Transphobic Culture

Liam Konemann

Inklings

For my parents.

Contents

Content Note

As comes with the territory of writing about a transphobic culture, please be aware that transphobia is detailed throughout *The Appendix,* in many ways and levels of detail, across the entire book.

Specific topics within that include:

Homophobic slurs (pages 14, 20, 61)
Murder (pages 15, 21, 26)
Rape (pages 15, 21, 26)
Sexual assault (page 21)
Transphobic slur (page 48)

Introduction

A Terrible Idea That Will Make You Sick

I was making the long trek back from the Royal Albert Hall.

I've long held the opinion that West London is a made-up place invented specifically to mess with me, but I was in a good mood anyway. I caught up with an old friend, the band we'd just seen were great, and I realised quite early on that there was an unknown bathroom just one floor up in the venue and I didn't need to queue for the loo all evening. I wasn't difficult to please.

It was late, but there were still a few mangled copies of a popular UK newspaper littered about the near-empty tube car. Flicking through one, I got to the arts pages and stopped at a review of Jeanette Winterson's *Frankissstein*, which I'd been thinking of picking up. I couldn't decide whether I wanted it enough to slightly inconvenience myself by having to read it in hardback, or if I should just wait for the paperback to come out like everybody else.

Foolishly, I thought the review might help me.

The first sentence or so was innocuous enough. But partway through, the reviewer got to the bit they really wanted to highlight. When revealing that Ry, *Frankisssstein*'s main character, is transgender, they wrote, 'of course!' You could practically feel the eye-roll coming through the newsprint. I knew then I was going to have to add the review to the growing list of transphobia I was keeping on my phone, but even *I* was surprised at the turn the next paragraph took. I actually caught sight of myself reflected in the carriage windows opposite, my mouth gaping open like a shocked clown. My good mood evaporated.

I hadn't drunk that much, but I took a picture of the review anyway so I could check it again in the morning. Maybe I misread it or was overreacting. I hoped it couldn't possibly be as bad as it seemed in the moment.

The next day, in between waking up and getting into the shower, I opened up the photograph of the review, standing there in the bathroom with my phone in one hand and a bottle of shower gel in the other. I re-read the piece while I waited for the water to heat up. I was right the first time. The newspaper really had described Ry like this:

S/he is called Ry, short for Mary (as in Mary Shelley), which makes you wonder why s/he isn't called Ree, so as not to sound like Ryan. S/he started out female and has XY chromosomes, but has had upper body surgery, no prosthetics and testosterone supplements which gives Ry an elongated clitoris – two centimetres, I think – and a satisfactory sex life.

An 'elongated clitoris'. Space in the arts pages of print newspapers is famously at a premium, meaning what gets reviewed – and who gets to review it – is hugely competitive. Imagine surmounting all of that, reading an entire novel, and then wasting three of your precious, finite words, commenting on the protagonist's clitoris.

The little aside, '– two centimetres, I think –', was almost comical. Here is the reviewer, sitting at their computer, painstakingly typing their query – 'trans clitoris how long' – into Google. One finger at a time, pecking out the letters with a furrowed brow. They would write the review and edit it, cutting out lines and phrases to meet the word count, and ultimately decide that their newfound knowledge of clitoris length absolutely *had* to stay. Presumably, multiple editors and sub-editors also decided it was necessary. The people of London needed to know what Ry's genitalia looked like. How else could they be sure if the book was any good?

Aside from the frankly bizarre interest in the quality of a fictional trans character's sex life, it was the dehumanising, almost moralising tone that struck me most. Nobody else in the media that I saw had referred to Ry as 'S/he'. In the promotional blurbs for *Frankissstein*, as well as in other reviews, Ry is always 'they'. Or, sometimes, just Ry. But whoever was covering the book at this particular publication had to make sure their readers understood that they personally weren't quite clear on what, exactly, the character was. They would not deign to dignify the character through use of the singular 'they'. They simply would not stand for it. Ry's fictional body was crossing the boundaries of what they considered acceptable, and this reviewer would not allow them to get away with it.

In comparison with the other items on my list, this review wasn't especially hateful. That was what made me so tired. The ugliness would rear its head in otherwise unsuspecting places. By now, I was so used to the media treating trans people as though we were delusional or dangerous that I'd inured myself to it. So, when someone wrote about people like me as though we were freakish, or just plain weird, it caught me off guard. It was like, *Oh, yeah. You don't think of me as quite human, do you?*

The review was added to my list, but I didn't open the document again that day. I left it the next day, too, and then next, and then weeks passed and I realised I was done. It had exhausted me. I felt othered, under siege. I had to stop.

The Appendix was over.

*

I don't remember having the idea. I think it came to me in stages, surfacing like fragments of a dream, but I couldn't say for sure.

The headlines had been building up, and at some point it seemed like we had to be approaching critical mass, but there's always doubt with these things. A distrust in your own senses. Is it really so bad? Or is the fact that you can't go two days without hearing about some new piece of hate just the amplification of an echo chamber? It could have been down to social media – I lost hours to the doom-scroll, clicking on handle after handle of increasingly more bigoted tweeters as though I was hoping to eventually reach the Big Boss. British transphobia's Patient Zero. This process yielded nothing. Eventually I would get a grip and put down the phone or close my laptop, feeling unwelcome in the world.

Part of me needed to prove – even just to myself – that what I felt was true. That I wasn't overreacting, being too sensitive, or imagining the volume of hatred both overt and insidious. I wanted to have something to point to as tangible proof. It seemed like a perfectly reasonable idea: when I came across a transphobic headline, comment, or news piece, I would add it to a list. I would file it by date, and note the outlet as well as any other key information, and then I would have inarguable evidence that I was right to be hurt.

To keep some sense of scientific integrity around the project, I had to set some boundaries. If I heard a rumour about something, or saw it hinted at on social media, I couldn't go looking for it like I had previously. I was not allowed to Google anything, or deliberately read papers and columnists I knew to be transphobic. There would be no doom-scrolling. Anything that made the list had to come my way organically, in the natural movements of my day-to-day life.

On the first day, Monday, I recorded four headlines. By Wednesday, I had eight entries. There were the head-lines, and a transphobic comment or two. There was also a tweet from an Australian rugby league player, who had shared a screenshot of a new story about one state making the gender on birth certificates optional, with the caption 'The devil has blinded so many people in this world, REPENT and turn away from your evil ways.'

It was an unpleasantly strong start.

As the list got longer, I came to think of it, privately, as 'The Appendix'. Appendix to what, I wasn't sure. But it helped me to think this was in service of something bigger. More journalistic.

In hindsight, my new project was probably a symptom of my old anxiety. The urge to know things for sure, to identify and catalogue potential threats, always rears its head at times of stress. Was I stressed in the Spring of 2019? At the time I would have said no more so than usual, but it's easy to see the correlation now. There were plenty of signs that my mental health wasn't exactly robust.

That March, I spent a chunk of my savings on a week in New York, where I hoped to distract myself from the sad state of my personal life and come home restored, refreshed. The turbulence on the flight out, however, was so bad that I spent four of the eight hours completely rigid in my seat, gripping the armrests and breathing hard. When the plane suddenly dropped altitude, the girl behind me screamed, her meal tray flying past my elbow and three feet down the aisle. I looked down at the sad, wilted piece of lettuce next to my shoe, trying to dissuade myself that it was going to be one of the last things I ever saw. I really didn't want to die staring at someone else's depressing salad.

Safely back on land, in the cab to the hotel, the novelty of being in America for the first time was overshadowed by the flotsam of adrenaline still floating around in my system. My body was convinced something terrible was about to happen. I woke up in the night with a shout, the image of a man standing over my bed dissolving in front of my eyes. It turned out to be the TV. The rest of the holiday was no more relaxing. The residual stress made me sick and I spent the best part of two days in bed. I was glad to have paid extra for a decent hotel.

Back in London, the hyper-alertness didn't settle. It simply re-directed itself into a preoccupation with the current of transphobia in the British press, which I had long tried to keep at a mental distance.

It wasn't something I wanted to sit with. Part of this was because I had more pressing concerns when it came to being trans; I had hormones to source and regular blood tests to check that the hormones weren't damaging my kidneys or liver. I had one mental roster of places I could go that had adequate toilets, and another of places that only had urinals, or where the locks were always broken, or where instead of a cubicle door there was only a curtain. Another mental list itemised shops and brands who made clothes that would come in my size. And, in the back of my mind, there was always the amorphous, shifting roster of those who knew I was trans and those who didn't. I was busy with the logistics of actually navigating my trans body through the world, partly.

The other part of it was, I was hiding.

For years, I had tried not to look. To pretend that they weren't talking about me in those articles, to never scroll below the line, to change the channel or close the tab any time I sensed a debate coming on. Now I couldn't stop looking. The 'transgender debate' was everywhere. Even as I tried to tell myself it was only confined to those Twitter echo chambers, I knew that wasn't true. I saw the headlines in the newspapers. I heard the jokes on TV. In late 2019, months after I decided to end The Appendix project, there was at least one motion passed at a local Labour Party meeting which declared there were 'legitimate concerns' surrounding the sex-based rights of women as they related to the 'support and dignity' of trans people, framing the two as in inherent opposition.[1] It reminded me of an incident the previous year, when several members of my household had gone to a local meeting whose stated purpose had been 'open conversation' around women's prisons, children's protections and more. Reading between the lines, my friends sensed a transphobic ambush. Not being a member of the Labour Party, I stayed home, and was glad to have done so when my flatmates returned, bringing with them the only two other attendees to have spoken out in support of trans women. Sitting around our living room drinking tea, they looked angry, defeated and exhausted. Their frustration was palpable.

Even if it had all taken place solely online, it was unreasonable to think I could just avoid the 'debates'. For one thing, I write about pop culture for a number of publications, and almost everything I cover, I hear about online. For another, this is the 21st-century, so I can't just close the apps – my friends are in there, not just my opposers.

It's important to acknowledge that the articles weren't really talking about me. Not technically, anyway. Historically speaking, the public attack on transgender people is enacted through false and insulting narratives about trans women. They bear the brunt of the cruelty, take most of the fallout, and are most often tasked with defending against it. A study by Professor Paul Baker at Lancaster University, comparing the coverage of trans people in nine major UK newspapers in 2012 and 2018-9, found that in the year 2018-9, the words 'tran-swoman' and 'transwomen' appeared 31 and 38 times respectively. By contrast, 'transmen' appeared twice. Baker recorded no instances of the word 'transman'.[2]

The push against trans men is more subtle. While trans women are presented as sexual predators and deviants, trans men are presented as fragile or deluded women who have fallen foul of internalised misogyny – often framed as self-hating lesbians pushed into transition by a society intolerant of masculine-presenting women. We are also occasionally used as a cudgel by gender critical types, who insist that our comparative absence from these 'conversations' is not because of their rampant transmisogyny, but rather because our voices are being drowned out by domineering trans women. There are plenty of people who have written far more eloquently on the demonisation of trans women than I, but suffice to say that the suggestion they shout down the rest of the trans community is, of course, another lie.

The Appendix, I decided, would help. It would be a visual representation of the broad transphobia a single trans person can experience just by existing in the world, from casual instances to outright hatred, to show how exhausting and unrelenting it is. Maybe if I posted about it on Twitter when it was done, the few people I knew who insisted it was important to 'hear both sides' might reconsider their position. I wasn't going to just come in and suddenly solve transphobia, but at least I'd be able to demonstrate why I personally felt so defeated by it all the time.

Seeing it was bad enough – could writing it down really make me feel any worse? It was just a tally. I could make a note of the headline, the date, and move on. After an arbitrary length of time – I decided on three months – I would stop counting, bash out a little paragraph to go alongside it, and post it on Medium or Twitter. *Look how often you talk about us*, I would say. Its perspective would of course be limited by the fact that I am white, and male 'passing', but maybe it would help me to explain the unexplainable. A few people in my tiny corner of the internet might get some idea of what it's like to wake up and be transgender in this country, day after day after day. I really thought I could handle it.

I was wrong.

By the time I gave up on The Appendix following the *Frankisssstein* review, I began to understand two things that other trans writers already know; one, that paying close, deliberate attention to transphobia is a terrible idea that will make you sick and, two, that showing people where they make you bleed would not stop them from cutting you again. There was no benefit to me witnessing every moment of transphobia that came my way, and my anxious need to have all the evidence was only a compulsion that was exacerbating the issue. The cycle had to stop.

But there was one final, positive thing I decided when wrapping up The Appendix. I didn't want a life where transness was about shame. I no longer cared for a world where a body like mine was presented as both the crime and the punishment. I wanted it to be a site of joy instead.

Chapter 1
Stealth

I was thinking about Brandon Teena.

One of my eight housemates, drunk again, took up his new favourite place in the upstairs hall of our crumbling east London terraced house. My locked bedroom door bounced back and forth in its frame as he pounded on it from the outside.

'Liam!' he shouted. 'Wake up. Come out!'

I held my breath and rolled to face the window as quietly as possible. If he thought I wasn't home, he might give up and go away. He might leave me alone.

The banging got louder. So far, the keypad lock on the door was holding – its sturdiness unusual in a house where we regularly had to stick a steak knife into the boiler to turn it on – but it would give eventually if he really wanted it to. Just weeks before, we'd had to kick another door down when the lock got jammed, so I knew it was possible. It just depended on how committed he was.

It was so late. I was so tired.

'Liam! Are you a fag today?'

I'm not here, I thought. *The lock will hold. He will go away.*

'Are you going to be a faggot today?'

If he *did* want to get through the door, if it started to splinter or yield, I supposed I could climb out the window. My bedroom was on the first floor but there was a bit of roof jutting out below, and I could slide from there onto the ground. Then what? I would just be in our garden in my pyjamas. How many fences would I have to climb before I made it to the street – three? Four? And where would I go from there? It was early 2014, and I'd only been in the country for three months. There wasn't really anywhere I could just turn up in the middle of the night.

The door kept rattling. I could see the light from the hall coming in underneath.

'Wake up! Are you going to be a fag today?'

I shut my eyes and tried to breathe slowly.

In the last few weeks, the housemate that was trying to wake up the neighbourhood had developed a preoccupation with my arse. He wanted to know what I did with it. Someone had told him that I wasn't straight, and now he wanted to know about my arse and whether or not there was hair on my body, although what one had to do with the other, I wasn't sure – even now I'm none the wiser.

A few nights before his first midnight door-slamming, we were all hanging out together, getting stoned. It was April Fool's Day. Sitting halfway out the window, I clambered back in, handed the spliff to somebody else, and said I was off. My housemate grinned.

'Are you going to be gay today?' he asked.

It took me a second to realise I wasn't in on the joke. That I was supposed to feel reduced.

I winked at him.

'Only for you, darling,' I said.

I shut the door in his face while the others laughed. I assumed that was what started it.

He was still outside my bedroom door, and I was still thinking about Brandon Teena, a trans man murdered in Humboldt, Nebraska, in 1993.

When I came out as trans not long before my eighteenth birthday, *Boys Don't Cry* – the film about his rape and murder, starring Hilary Swank as Brandon in a role that won her the Oscar for Best Supporting Actress – was the only movie about a trans man that I could find. This was years before the quote-unquote transgender tipping point, when I regularly had to explain what the word even meant. I knew what the movie entailed, and I knew it was going to hurt to watch. But what else was there?

I had to look, if only for that briefest of moments, where the fictionalised Brandon stands in front of his bedroom mirror, winding an ace bandage around his chest to keep it flat. I'd never seen anyone else do that before. I rewound it and watched again. The way he turned side-on in the mirror to look at the flatness of his chest and check the bulge of a pair of rolled-up socks in his underwear. I watched him as if I was watching myself, standing there thinking, *Does this look natural?* The amount of mental effort I have expended over the years wondering if I looked natural.

Beyond that moment, part of me felt like I had to face the horror. The same instinct that years later would cause me to create The Appendix led me to believe that I had to see for myself the terrible things that could happen to someone like me. I had to know the exact shape of the worst possible endpoint and find somewhere to put the knowledge that it really could happen. That it really had happened to other people. The film underscored what I already knew; that my body was not always safe to live in.

There's a moment in the opening scene of *Boys Don't Cry* where Brandon's cousin, having just given him a haircut and now watching him stuff a sock down the front of his jeans, asks, 'So you're a boy. Now what?'

For me, there was only one answer: now get the hell out.

When I was first coming into my queerness, Queensland was not an ideal place to be. My British friends often seem to think of Australia as quite liberal, but Queensland especially is deeply conservative, historically speaking. The right to an abortion, for example, was only extended beyond risk-to-life cases in 2018. The age of consent for gay men was equalised in 2016, and equal marriage was passed in December the following year. Until then, married trans people were required to get a divorce if they wanted to change the gender listed on their birth certificate. These days, they only have to undergo reassignment surgery – for the trans men, a hysterectomy will do, so it seems the requirement is not proof of commitment to cisnormative genitalia, but rather sterilisation – and present statutory declarations from two doctors to prove it. How far we've come.

The birth certificate is a particular problem, given that in Australia it's common for employers to ask new hires to provide a copy as proof of citizenship.

At the time that I was going through it, it was slightly easier to change the gender on your driver's license. All you had to do for that was fill in a form, provide your proof of name change, and get a psychiatrist, psychologist or 'registered medical practitioner' to write a letter asserting that, *Yes, you are in fact the gender that you say you are*. Not long before I managed to complete these contortions, I was asked for ID at a checkout. I handed over my driver's license and the cashier frowned. She went to speak to her manager, taking my license with her. The manager obviously told her it was okay because she came back and handed it to me.

'Sorry,' she said. 'It's just because, you know...'

She'd thought it was forged because it said F instead of M, to which I wanted to point out that if it had been a fake, I'd probably have got the gender right.

None of this covers the social aspect, which, back then, required me to explain myself a lot. It was exhausting, and othering, and I felt like I could never be seen as myself. I was always two people – the boy I was, and the girl I used to be. I was so tired of never being fully accepted as one thing or the other. I wanted so badly to not be known as 'the trans guy'. I decided that when I left Australia, there would be no more of it. I would only be seen as myself, a fully formed person not on the way to or from anything. I moved to London as soon as I could. In the early 2010s, there was no way for me to predict that things would become so toxic in the UK almost a decade later.

For the best part of five years after arriving in London, I was very careful who I told I was trans. It's fairly likely that, unless we were very close friends, if you and I were not going to share a bed between the years 2013 and

2018, I never mentioned it. There are probably people in my life who will find out that I'm trans through the publication of this book. Sorry, guys.

The word 'stealth' has largely fallen out of favour now, implying as it does espionage and deception, but between the ages of about 21 and 25, that was how I thought of myself. I was in hiding. I wanted to be a regular guy, because to be trans was to be disturbing. Disturbed. It was as though I thought that if I could just do a convincing enough impression of a cis person for the outside world, I could actually become one. In hindsight, I was trying to side-step the loneliness and isolation that had accompanied me for most of my life. I wanted to assimilate. So I mostly kept quiet, and every time another trans person died, or there was a public debate about our rights, I swallowed it. I kept swallowing it, like microdosing cyanide to build up an immunity. By the time I realised it didn't work, that it was only making me sick, I turned around and realised I had no idea how to undo what I'd done. When is the right moment to tell a friend you've known for four years that you used to be a girl? You don't owe anyone your past, but for me, I reached a certain point where I wanted to be understood and accepted for exactly who I was.

There were other reasons not to tell people, too. I thought my friends would be okay, but every now and then somebody revealed themselves to be less safe than I had assumed. There was that housemate of mine, banging away on my bedroom door, and then there had been the co-worker in a Soho café, who told me he hated working there because of all the faggots. He told me that people had once set off nail bombs here, and that he wished they would again so the fags wouldn't get so confident and they'd all leave. It was 9pm, the café was closed, and nobody else was around. I felt a cold flush wash over my body and didn't tell him that I was one of the people he wanted blown up.

'So you're a boy. Now what?'

Now this. Now the realisation that no matter how hard you might try, you are still unable to conform. You can still be found out and hated for it.

With my homophobic housemate outside the door every few nights, I knew I was a far cry from the events depicted in *Boys Don't Cry*. I was not about to be brutalised the way that Brandon had been, but still the fear lingered. After all, one could only be so sure. Now that my transness was a secret, it was one I couldn't afford not to keep.

I wondered what would happen if my housemate caught me by surprise one night when he was in this sort of mood. Still under the guise of a joke, he might try to touch me. He would realise. Then what? I couldn't say.

There was no accounting for the way that surprised cis people reacted to trans bodies. I knew trans people who had been groped by strangers on buses and in other public places, touched in ways they did not consent to, by someone who wanted to find out what they were. Never 'who', always 'what'. These people never reported what happened to them. There was no point.

After Brandon was brutally raped by Tom Nissen and John Lotter – the two men who were his friends until they found out who he was, and who ultimately murdered him less than a week later – he reported it to the local sheriff's department. In the film, the attack itself is spliced in with the degrading police interview, one assault merging into another.

'When they got a spread of you, when they poked you, where'd they try to pop it in first at?' the fictionalised sheriff asks. Brandon, visibly shaking, cannot answer clearly. Can barely shape the word.

This, or something like it, really happened. Brandon's police interview is widely available online, and for about five minutes, Sheriff Charles Laux can be heard suggesting that perhaps he was a voluntary participant in his own rape. He appears to be more interested in what Brandon tries to explain as his 'sexual identity crisis'.

'Why do you run around with girls instead of, ah, guys, being you are a girl yourself? Why do you make girls think you're a guy?' the real Laux asks.

'I haven't the slightest idea,' says Brandon.

'You haven't the slightest idea. You go around kissing other girls?'

'The ones that I know that know about me.'

'What about the ones that don't know about you? Do you kiss them?'

Backed into this degrading position, Brandon gamely asks, 'What does that have to do with what happened last night?'

But Laux doesn't let it go.

'Because I'm trying to get some answers so I know exactly what's going on. Now, do you want to answer that question for me or not?'

'I don't see why I have to,' says Brandon.

He's aiming for defiance, but his voice is small.

The sheriff tells him that the question is going to come up in court, and that he should have an answer now.

'See what I'm saying?' says Laux.

But the question never came up in court. It never came up, and neither did anything else, because the sheriff and his team never bothered to make an arrest. The tape cuts off after Laux asks Brandon to explain his 'sexual identity crisis'.

Brandon says, 'I don't know if I can even talk about it.'

Then there is silence.

Six days later, he was dead.

The cops' disinterest in Brandon's case never came as a surprise to me, for the same reason that trans people I knew never reported the random sexual assaults they experienced. We had been on the receiving end of their bigotry ourselves or had heard of enough people who had.

When I was eighteen, a policeman threatened to take me into a van and strip search me to figure out whether I was a boy or a girl.

I was driving to work, and I was going to be late. I got pulled over for a random roadside breath test. After I pulled into the bay with the other cars, the cop came up to my window and asked if I'd drunk any alcohol in the last twenty-four hours or taken any drugs in the last seven days. Then he took my license – which had an M on it by this point – did his tests and walked away.

It was the kind of generic, brilliant blue day that tends to bleed into all the others in south-east Queensland. The state's slogan was *Beautiful One Day, Perfect The Next.* It was true enough, so long as you were a very specific type of person.

The cop came back to my window and asked about my previous name. He wanted to know who this person was, the former identity who was now a footnote on the government records. He didn't bother to keep his voice down. I was hyper-aware of the people in the next car, their open window less than a metre away from mine.

'That was me,' I said. 'From before. I'm transgender.'

'It's still there on our system,' he said. 'And it also says female.'

'I don't know what to tell you,' I said. 'I went to the Department of Transport and changed it.'

He knew that, of course, because he was holding my perfectly valid new license in his hand. Their system would always indicate that I had changed my name and gender, just like my reissued birth certificate still listed the name I was born with on the back page. Legally, there was no way for me to pretend this identity never existed. He wasn't alerting me to an error and we both knew it.

'Well, it's still showing that identity, so there's a conflict.'

I waited.

'Do you have any drugs on you, or in the vehicle?'

'No,' I said.

'Are you sure?'

'Yes.'

He pointed out the on-site testing van.

'Because of what's on our system, if I wanted to, I could take you in there and strip search you,' he said. 'Do you understand?'

The people in the next car were still right there, trying too conspicuously to look as though they weren't listening.

'Yes,' I said. 'I understand.'

He handed me back my license. Both the drug and alcohol tests, of course, had come back clear.

See what I'm saying?

Years later, I wished that I had reported him. That I had stood up for myself, had taken his name, or could even just remember his face. But he was just a cop. He was just a middle-aged guy in Brisbane in 2011, and he could have been anyone.

*

My housemate wasn't getting tired. He was still outside the door, still shouting, and I wanted to go to sleep, or be somewhere else, or just be left alone. It didn't seem like that much to ask. Finally, one of the others came to the door.

'Leave him alone man, come on,' he said.

They went back and forth a few times before they went away. I still couldn't sleep. It wasn't until the next day that I realised they'd been speaking English the whole time, despite the fact that they shared a mother tongue. They never spoke to each other in English. I still have no idea if it was because the second housemate wanted me to know I was being defended, or because the whole thing was an elaborate wind-up. We never talked about it.

*

After the murder trial, there was a subsequent case in which Brandon Teena's mother sued Sheriff Laux for negligence. In the eventual final ruling, the Chief Justice John Henry found that Laux's tone in the interview was 'demeaning, accusatory and intimidating.' He said Laux referred to Brandon as 'it' and was more interested in his sexuality than the rape case at hand. The *ABC News* reportage on the verdict called Brandon 'a cross-dressing woman.' Neither Tom Nissen nor John Lotter were ever charged with Brandon's rape.

Even though years had passed since Brandon's murder and the release of *Boys Don't Cry,* this was how the climate looked when I came out. I absorbed the idea that I was only accepted within my little circle, and that everyone else must be kept in the dark at all costs. It went on like this for years. Every time I was on the receiving end of someone's homophobia, like when my housemate was getting worked up about the fact that I liked men, I thought, *What would happen if you knew the rest?* I trusted almost no-one. But this was what I wanted when leaving Australia, even when I didn't want it anymore. I was unknown.

Chapter 2

Won't Somebody *Please* Think of the Children?

I had been an unknown for a long time.

Trans people who keep quiet about it are professional revisionists. The gender markers in stories change, ages move around, you have no pictures. You find yourself telling tiny, pointless lies. You tell people you played different sports, you wore different clothes, had an entirely different life. Unlike some trans men, I never identified as a lesbian, which is significant only in that instead of inventing a series of steadily less believable fictional high school girlfriends, I moved my coming out story forward about seven or eight years.

'What was it like being gay at school?' people would ask, and I would say, 'Yeah, fine.'

There are all sorts of ways of being queer, even if you can't name it at the time.

In his memoir *Fathers and Sons*, Howard Cunnell writes about the night he and his wife learned why their child couldn't stop screaming. 'For a long time Araba and I had believed Jay was gay, and that in time she would tell us so,' he says.[1] This is a fairly common experience when it comes to parents of trans youths. The afternoon I came out, standing in my front door as my Dad left to go home, I said, 'You're not surprised, are you?'

He shrugged. 'When you were a kid I used to tell people you were going to be a lesbian cult leader.'

Close enough.

But Jay, of course, is not gay. As he realises, Cunnell writes that his son was carrying something for which there were no words. That Jay knew something nobody else in the world knew. It can be a burden, this knowing.

It's hard to say if I was a transgender kid. Like Jay, it wasn't something I had language for. Do we consider children transgender only if they know the specific, medical term for what they are?

In recent years in the UK, questions like these have been at the heart of the transgender 'debate'. Parents, doctors and advocates – not to mention the actual kids themselves – say that allowing children to grow up in the right gender, with the right support, leads to overwhelmingly positive outcomes.[2] Transgender children who feel their identities are supported and affirmed by their families have better mental health outcomes than those who don't; they report higher levels of life satisfaction, have greater self-esteem, and are less likely to abuse substances, and consider or attempt suicide.[3][4][5] But the opposing side – which includes 'gender critical' anti-trans campaigners (and, similarly, for some unfathomable reason, comedy writers such as Graham Linehan[6] and Robert Webb[7], who simply could not ignore a fabricated issue that has no effect on them whatsoever) – have argued along the lines that affirming children who want to transition is tantamount to conversion therapy.[8][9][10] These campaigners often claim that 'trans activists' (the name they give to trans people who want to, you know, be allowed to live their lives) force adult decisions onto children. They are wilfully ignorant of the fact that removing the provision of gender-affirming pathways by blocking trans children from care *is* forcing them onto an irreversible path – that of an unwanted puberty, and a body that will later be harder to change.

It's true that many gender non-conforming kids don't grow up to transition. But there is also no great push to convince them that they have to. This is what gender identity services are for; to allow young people who are struggling to find the time and space to figure these feelings out for themselves. The eventual transition of many kids who use these services doesn't prove that they are being pushed in that direction, but rather that they were diagnosed correctly in the first place. You cannot make a gay kid trans, just like nobody could ever turn me into a lesbian, no matter how many times the world told me that that must have been what I was.

I could list all the times I knew I was a boy. I could start writing and never stop, unfurl an endless scroll of memories and moments as evidence that trans children exist, that I am who I say I am and always have been, but it wouldn't translate. People who seek to debunk the existence of trans identity often point to the times people have said that they liked Barbie dolls though, to the world, they looked like a boy. Or they liked football even though they were considered a girl. This is meant to be proof that we transition because of cultural stereotypes around gender, which we then supposedly perpetuate. But how to express the inexpressible? Consider Cunnell's son and all his screaming. The truth for which there was no language. You cannot expect a child to be able to tell you why they are the way that they are; they can only tell you that they are.[11]

One of the many problems that surround these decisions, the separating of who's trans from who's not, is that distress is considered more indicative than joy. While we are gradually moving towards a less medicalised, more flexible view of gender identity, transition pathways are often predicated on pain. If this is the basis for the wider narrative around transness – the assumption that all trans people seek medical transition and all people who transition do so because of an otherwise unmanageable pain – then in the public perception transness becomes a sort of curse.

For nearly a decade after I came out as trans, the official name for the underlying condition of transness was Gender Identity Disorder. When it was finally changed, so that trans people were no longer viewed as mentally ill purely for being trans, 'gender dysphoria' became the new official term. It's a diagnostic label, a name for the distress arising from conflict between your internal gender and your appearance or the way you are perceived by the world, and not everyone with gender dysphoria is trans. However, for most trans people seeking gender-affirming pathways, a diagnosis of gender dysphoria can prove necessary. Access to care, then, seems to hinge on whether or not a person is in enough pain to be transgender.

It would be ridiculous to suggest that trans people don't experience distress, of course – there's pain and confusion, and an absolutely profound sense of aloneness and difference, but it's not the whole experience.

Although Howard Cunnell is writing from the perspective of a parent and not a trans person, there's a tiny moment in *Fathers and Sons* that beautifully and simply depicts the phenomenon of gender euphoria – the incomparable joy of being recognised for what you are.

'Sometimes when he was small he'd be called as a boy, long hair and all, and he'd smile, secret, shy,' he writes.

I've underlined that passage in my copy. Every time I read it I want to underline it again. *There it is. The first time I saw myself completely mirrored in a book.* I remember those secret, shy smiles.

*

Late '90s. I think it's summer. I'm about six, seven at a push. I'm staying at my friend's house for the weekend, and his mum has let us ride our bikes down to the park unsupervised. My parents would freak. There are bark chips covering the ground, dappled light is falling through the gum trees above our heads. I'm wearing my prized Scooby Doo baseball cap. These memories are always cinematic. Idyllic.

I have no idea the internet exists yet.

As we approach the narrow bridge that crosses the dry creek leading into the park, a father and his small son ride up from the other direction.

'Wait here and let these boys pass,' the father says, and I feel it.

Something inside me is singing. *These boys*, I think.

These boys, these boys, these boys. He saw.

In another memory, one or two years later, it is night and my parents are checking us into a caravan park at the southern edge of the world. They're talking to the owner, and she smiles down at me and says something about 'him'. My parents smile too and don't correct her, but I am so bright and shy, practically fizzing, that she realises.

'Oh, I'm sorry!' she says.

My mum waves a hand.

'Oh, don't be,' she says. 'She wants to be a boy. You've made her day.'

Twenty years later, these moments feel formative. I take them out and turn them over, wearing them smooth and burnishing their gold. Would they have proved that I was trans then? If my family and I knew that trans people existed, could we have taken these talismans to the doctor and said, *How about this then?* Or would they have asked only about my pain?

*

As Cunnell looks back at his son's childhood in his memoir, he casually dismantles many of the myths that surround the lives of trans children. He and his wife's assumption that Jay would grow up to be a lesbian flies in the face of those who suggest children are being pushed into transition by homophobic parents, for one. Their obvious acceptance of Jay's potential homosexuality, and eventual transgender identity, also lead me to the question I often ask when such an argument is made: what makes these people believe that we live in a world in which a parent would be so homophobic as to reject a gay child, but would welcome a trans one with open arms?

Anti-trans campaigners often claim that parents are being met with the question, 'Wouldn't you rather have a daughter than a gay son?' This is rather disingenuous phrasing. The key detail is not 'a daughter' but 'a *trans* daughter'. Of course, in an ideal world parents would be equally delighted with all hypothetical children, whether trans or cis, gay or straight, but we are considering an imaginary scenario in which they are being forced to choose, so it's important to present the fictitious choice for what it is. It is a blatant attempt to position trans lives in opposition to gay ones, and to poison the well of queer solidarity. Howard's telling pushes against a narrative of rejection, and instead presents the truth of unconditional love. He sets it out simply, as he watches his wife comfort their child:

'But Araba won't let go, not until Jay tells and somewhere, wherever she is, Jay knows this. Jay can't say anything that will stop her mother loving her. Araba will sit holding her all night if she has to, while Jay screams like someone dying or being born.'

Later that same night, after Jay has finally told,

Howard goes in to see him.

'I recognise Jay again,' he writes. 'He seems so sad to be back. Jay looks at me, and I realise he's frightened, like I'm going to tell him off. I hug him.

'It's OK Jay, I say, it's OK. And though I understand nothing of what has happened, I say: "It'll be all right Bear. I'm sorry you feel so bad, but it'll be all right."'

Howard also makes clear through small, seemingly inconsequential moments, that Jay knows himself. Neither he nor Araba ever suggests that, at thirteen years old, he is too young to be trans.

A UK High Court ruling at the end of 2020 that said young people are 'highly unlikely' to be able to give informed consent to things like puberty blockers,[11] hinges on this claim. It's yet another false argument that trans people can't win. If you say you're a different gender to what you appear as a child, you're told you'll grow out of it. *It's a phase, it's fleeting, you don't understand.* If you say it as a teenager, well, it's hormones. *It's puberty, you're confused,* or *You're not ready to grow up and become a woman yet so you wish you were a boy instead.* So, then, you shut up and you're an adult, and you're twenty-five, thirty, thirty-five, and you come out again, finally, and someone says: *Well, you can't possibly be transgender, can you? You'd have said something by now.*

Chapter 3
The Appendix

It's strange, looking back. As a child, of course I had absolutely no concept of transphobia, but I understood transness in implicit terms. I knew I should have been a boy, and somewhere along the line something got messed up, and I wasn't one – at least, not to anyone but me. But I didn't understand that I was carrying a characteristic that would be the target of such public vitriol later – that would be painted as misogyny, foolishness and delusion – and yet I knew I couldn't tell people the truth. It didn't seem like the kind of thing I could ever adequately explain.

When I began The Appendix in 2019, much of the media coverage around trans people centred on children. This is classic moral panic territory. Those seeking to restrict and oppress groups or behaviour that they deem deviant or immoral often begin by arguing that their opponents present a danger to the healthy development of kids, or to childhood innocence. It's a rhetoric that has been used widely for years, cropping up not only in conversations about LGBT+ rights, when it lead to the introduction of Section 28 in 1988,[1] but also to oppose things like explicit lyrics in rock music, which led to the introduction of 'parental advisory' stickers on albums labelled obscene.[2] Now, it was trans peoples' turn to be framed as a risk to the youth.

There were 'concerns'. On the day that I started making a record of transphobia in earnest, the headlines in *The Times* ran like this:

CALLS TO END TRANSGENDER
'EXPERIMENT ON CHILDREN'[3]

FAMILIES 'EXPLOITED BY GENDER LOBBY GROUPS
PUSHING FOR TREATMENT'[4]

DOUBTS OVER EVIDENCE FOR USING DRUGS
ON THE YOUNG[5]

IT FEELS LIKE CONVERSION THERAPY FOR
GAY CHILDREN, SAY CLINICIANS[6]

This is one newspaper, on *one* day. It was as if *The Times* had seen the special edition issues *NME* put out covering a single band in forensic detail and thought, *What if we did that, but for the transgenders? Oh, won't somebody* please *think of the children?*

At the risk of sounding like a broken record, what about the trans children? Looking at the headlines as an adult, with a past and a childhood I was now struggling to access in any meaningful way, all I could think was that these people had no idea. No idea about families, childhoods, or health needs like mine. No idea about the fundamental difference between being a gay child and being a trans one, let alone the fact that people could be both. But the moral panic isn't, really and truly, about children having identities that some factions don't think they can have. The children are the straw man. The real 'concern' is trans adults, those exploitative 'gender lobby groups pushing for treatment'. There seems to be this belief – however disingenuous – that trans people are out here trying to convert people to our cause, building up some kind of bizarre transsexual army to mount a co-ordinated attack on the rights of women and gays.

These are the well-worn themes that get wheeled out time and time again. When the headlines refer to trans children, they are filled with hand-wringing over the rate of transition in what they see as confused young girls who want to become boys. These are young lesbians, they say, or simply tomboys who are being traumatised by a society in which the expectations of what women and girls can be is so rigid that it leaves no room for individuality or difference. There is, of course, enough truth in the latter half of this assertion that any reasonable person might be inclined to agree with the whole of it. Lesbians and masculine or gender non-conforming women of all kinds face enormous societal prejudice. That's not in contention, but there is no evidence that these young people are being forced into transition on a mass scale, and charities and Gender Identity services have stated time and time again that their purpose is not to steer, but to provide space for understanding. The Gender Identity Development Service, a 'highly specialised clinic for young people presenting with difficulties with their gender identity', specify on their webpage that they see both young people who feel uncomfortable with their birth gender, as well as those who feel constrained with the gender roles enforced by society. Similarly, Mermaids, the charity dedicated to supporting gender-diverse people up to the age of twenty, assure parents visiting their site that they provide assistance for young people who choose to transition and those who don't.

'Supporting your child doesn't mean they'll take a particular direction or follow a particular medical pathway, like hormone therapy or gender affirming surgeries. [...] At Mermaids, we believe in allowing young people to make the right choices for them, without feeling any pressure to be what others might expect them to be. We have supported countless kids over the years and each and every one of them has followed their own unique path,' their page states.[7]

When the headlines refer to trans adults, it's a different story.

So much of transphobia is rooted in the gatekeeping of womanhood. In 2020, the news said both MOTHER WHO CALLED TRANS WOMAN 'HE' ON TWITTER IS CLEARED OF WRONGDOING AFTER APPEALING AGAINST CONVICTION[8] and WOMEN SLAM TAMPAX OVER TWEET CELEBRATING THE 'DIVERSITY OF ALL PEOPLE WHO BLEED' AMID CALLS FOR BOYCOTT. [9]

The door is locked from both sides. Nobody in, nobody out.

Looking at the headlines in recent years, all those young women the gender criticals worry about, the ones whose transitions were supposedly fuelled by unyielding conventions of girlhood and sexism, miraculously disappear at the age of eighteen. They give way to huge, unfathomable quantities of 'men' wanting to become women, supposedly beguiled by those self-same gender roles which it was previously argued nobody could possibly want to live within. The argument becomes partly about bathroom and refuge provision: where is it safe for trans women to pee? Where can they sleep when there is nowhere else?

In these cases, far from being presented as the disproportionately vulnerable group that they are, trans women become the shadowy threat. The faux-concern about lesbians crops up here too, in the argument that trans women are tricking lesbians into sleeping with them, or that lesbians are afraid to reject trans women for fear of being labelled transphobic. Coupled with the assertion that trans men are butch lesbians being brainwashed into transition by heteronormative forces, the headline becomes;

LESBIANS FACING EXTINCTION AS
'TRANSGENDERISM' BECOMES PERVASIVE.[10]

I'm mixing my timelines a little now, I'll admit. That one's from December 2020. *The Telegraph*, this time.

The difficulty about writing this now, a few years later, is that I cannot easily separate the entries of The Appendix from the climate that still persists. There's no conclusion. It all gets mixed in together – pull one thread, and a tangle of other issues follow. At the outset of this project, it was my plan to look back on The Appendix as a closed period of my life. I wanted to write about Graham Linehan's claims in *The Irish Independent* on the 7th of April 2019 that he is 'not transphobic and never [has] been', in which the author of the article stated that Linehan had been caught up in controversy over 'something that a majority of people are still confused about… the rights and demands of transsexual people',[11] as if we were hostage takers calling for a million dollars and a getaway car, and not just people asking that other people leave us alone. I wanted to write about John Boyne's 2019 young adult novel *My Brother's Name is Jessica*, how he claimed to have done extensive research about trans lives and taken great pains to write a sensitive and authentic novel, and yet somehow still managed to get it all wrong right there in the book's title. And then he kept going.

During the book's publication week, which fell in the middle of The Appendix project, Boyne wrote an article for *The Irish Times*:

WHY I SUPPORT TRANS RIGHTS BUT
REJECT THE TERM 'CIS'.[12]

'Cis' is only a prefix, drawn from Latin and meaning 'on this side'. It sits opposite the Latin prefix 'trans', meaning 'on the other side of; across; beyond'. The position Boyne set out in his article, that 'cis' is an unwanted term forced upon others by trans people,[13] is similar to that of many gender critical radical feminists, who as a group have written on the subject fairly extensively.[14][15][16] Whether he meant to or not, the author was giving airtime to a claim that has been used to paint trans people as ideological aggressors who are seeking to recategorise others and erode the terms 'man' and 'woman' – and by extension, women's rights and the existence of homosexuality.

The article set off a wave of debate on social media and in the press. My Appendix entry for the following day reads only '~debate~ on twitter about whether the term 'cis' is offensive'. I noted it down quickly at my desk at work, not wanting to dedicate any sort of real time to breaking down each and every article, post and quote-tweet that made up the maelstrom. If I had, The Appendix entry for that day would have been a near-indecipherable tangle, a sort of rat-king of hot-takes and comment pieces. It would have said something like:

*Twitter user X quote-tweets Boyne
article to say how bad it is*

Twitter user Y replies to X, also to say how bad it is

Twitter user Z quote-tweets Y, makes further comment

*Twitter user A screenshots a follow-up article about why
Boyne is right and tweets it, adds disparaging comment
about the piece*

*Twitter user X replies to A with
eye-rolling emojis, retweets*

And so on. The problem here is not the original piece, or at least not entirely. The issue is that every article about trans people, every negative or clumsy statement, sets off an avalanche of further comments and coverage. Some of this happens on Twitter, and when it does I always feel a complicated mix of emotions. Often there is relief at knowing that I am not alone, am not going insane, and that a particular article or statement really is egregious. There is comfort and happiness in knowing that I have many friends, both online and off, who would step up to the plate and challenge transphobia when they see it. Inevitably, though, there is also discomfort. Irritation. Depression. In April 2019, regardless of the fact that people were condemning or dismantling Boyne's statement and the book it was promoting, I still had to see the initial affront over and over again. In 2020 and 2021, many people now seem to realise the possible ill-effects of sharing transphobia onto trans people's time-lines, even to disparage it – at least, most of the people I follow do, although that may be down to my robust Twitter muted words list, which now prevents me from seeing anything that includes most words and acronyms related to transphobia in addition to more innocuous irritations, such as any tweet featuring the phrases 'Baby Yoda', 'Ms Rona' or 'Tom Holland's Lip Sync'.

Of course, once again the issue isn't localised to Twitter, or any other social media platform. An article like WHY I SUPPORT TRANS RIGHTS BUT REJECT THE TERM ‘CIS’ and its community pushback inevitably spawns other articles. In this case, the comment pieces dragged on for the next month and a half. *The Spectator* read:

THE AUTHOR JOHN BOYNE IS WRONG TO PANDER TO TRANS ACTIVISTS[17]

Spiked went with:

JOHN BOYNE IS A MAN, NOT A CIS MAN[18]

Both of these, naturally, kicked off their own Twitter deluges (which I've kept anonymised to avoid contributing to the discourse avalanche): 'Never, ever in a million years will I use [cis]. It's nothing to do with identity. It's to do with power. Don't play their game.' 'The trans "lobby" don't want to call normal men/women "normal", as that would imply that transsexual people are "not normal", so they came up with using "Cis" to refer to normal men/women to avoid the uncomfortable highlighting that they themselves are not normal.' 'Don't change your speech to try to satisfy the delusions of these mentally ill people.' 'WTF is a "cis" anyhow? I'm a woman plain and simple. I'm not "cis" anything.' 'What if I find the term cis offensive? I am a woman end of story.'

It went on like this for days.

All of these I lumped under the umbrella of that same '~debate~' when it came to The Appendix. As it barrelled on, this particular entry had less and less to do with the original event, and more to do with how a single incident becomes a sort of Hydra, a many-headed monster of transphobia and hurt.

This is not to say that the original article didn't bother me. It was frustrating, more than anything. The author's insistence that he is not a 'cis man' but rather just 'a man' suggests a misunderstanding of the term at best, and at worst a deliberate othering.

It's worth noting that under this argument, trans people are not given the option of being simply 'men' or 'women'. What such a position implies, as even some who hold it acknowledge, is: *I'm normal, and you're the ones who need a qualifier.* It's like writing an article saying WHY I SUPPORT GAY RIGHTS BUT REJECT THE TERM 'STRAIGHT'. The purpose of the term 'cisgender', like the purpose of the term 'heterosexual', is to communicate that the other identities or orientations are not deviance, but rather possibilities within the normal range of human experience. No one is more valid or normal than the other.

As the discussion spiralled on, I blocked and I muted and I logged off, and then I walked over and over into transphobia elsewhere.

While social media is undeniably a hotbed of vitriol and bad faith arguments, a lot of people seem to mistakenly think that this means transphobia lives and dies there. The assumption seems to be that these platforms are toxic, and if you walk away from them, the venom is gone. If you are experiencing the exhausting, all-pervasive onslaught of opinions around trans lives, it's because you are looking for it, or putting yourself in spaces where it is likely to be discussed. This is why it was crucial that the original iteration of The Appendix only included entries that I came across organically, so I could show definitively that it doesn't make a scrap of difference.

Outside of Twitter there was, of course, the Jeanette Winterson review. But there was also news coming out of America that Iowa had banned Medicaid for gender-affirming surgeries, that Donald Trump had banned trans people from openly serving in the military, that a girl was expelled from her high school for fighting back after seven cis boys stormed into the girls' bathroom 'in protest' at a trans boy being allowed to use the correct facilities. That Spring, Armenian MPs were calling for trans activists to be burned alive. The front page of the *Scotsman* said: SNP MINISTERS URGE CAUTION OVER SEX 'DEFINITION CHANGE.'[19] A former editor of *The Times* was suing the publication for transphobic bullying. A friend who didn't know I'm trans used the word 'tranny' in casual conversation, and then a week later I walked through my own living room as my flatmate laughed at a TV show using the same word.

I wanted to ask everybody I came across what they all thought they were playing at. I felt hyper-vigilant, constantly on alert for the comments and the cruelty. I was tired all the time. I was sad. I had started to believe the things that were said about us.

For a while, I considered also including the transphobic dating app messages I received in The Appendix, but soon the list became far too unwieldy, and I had to take most of them off. Suffice to say, I was receiving a lot of offers of impregnation during that time in my life.

One message I did include was from a man telling me I should smile more. When I told him to go away, he replied, 'Boys wind each other up, better get used to it.' I ignored him, but I remember how it bothered me – the instruction to 'smile', such a common refrain from misogynists everywhere and so clearly rooted in his view of me as female, confirmed by his follow-up declaration that I'd better get used to it, as if I was brand new to masculinity and needed to be educated as to what it is 'boys' do. As if boys as a species are all the same, and there are in fact right and wrong ways to perform maleness. It felt like an odd position, coming as it did from a gay man, but as a group even we aren't immune to the creep of toxic masculinity, even as many of us are cast out by it.

There are plenty of things I could tell this man about boys. I could tell him how my group of – cis, straight – friends and I say 'hello darling' when we meet and yell 'love you' when we leave. That we wind each other up, constantly, relentlessly – in person and via text and in the provision of utterly nonsense birthday gifts and holiday souvenirs – and that somebody also told us that we compliment each other more than any other group of people they've ever known. This is what boys do, too.

When I think about joy, I think of my friends.

All of this was true then too, of course, but during those months the bright spots were hard to hold on to in a social climate that made me feel as I had when I was keeping my trans identity a secret; that outside of the people who loved me most, I was unwelcome. A burden.

*

I came out of this period slowly. When wrapping up the initial Appendix I'd made the decision to embrace my transness, but in hindsight this process was an exercise in false starts. As early as July 2019 I began to think more closely about the factors that had spurred me to collate The Appendix in the first place, and wondered what, if anything, I could take from it. I thought maybe there was something to be said about the rejection of shame, or about the futility of 'witnessing' the way I'd tried to do, but I wasn't sure. There was a gulf I couldn't get around. Despite my intentions, I still wasn't engaging with transness and transmasculinity in any meaningful way. I'd just decided to be happy with it, and considered the job done. It seemed like a positive step at the time, but I hadn't really done any work on building a foundation for joy. I just announced to myself that I felt it.

You can, sometimes, trick yourself into joy. Given enough time, I think my surface-level contentment with my transness would have deepened naturally. I was gaining confidence in myself as a queer man and took pleasure in that part of my identity, and as I made more queer friends, read more trans books, and worried less about seeming 'too queer' or being 'too much', it seems likely that I would have got there eventually. But towards the end of 2019 and the start of 2020 I was still in the early stages, and a thing like joy can be so fragile.

I hadn't built the kind of house that would hold up in a storm, and a storm was on the horizon.

Chapter 4
Not 'Born This Way'

The trouble with trans joy these days is that it's difficult to keep burning. Sooner or later, some 'debate' or other comes along and kills your vibe. It would be nice to be able to say that while I felt under siege for several months while collating The Appendix back in 2019, reluctant to turn on the TV or look at the newspapers lined up in the supermarket, bracing myself every time I opened the internet, once I got through those few months it never happened again.

I wanted to be able to neatly wrap up this project and say, 'All this made me want to die once, but it's over now.' But it isn't over. The *Telegraph* headline about lesbians facing extinction, from December 2020, is still not an outlier. Throughout 2020, as if things weren't bad enough in the world due to the COVID-19 pandemic, anti-trans campaign groups redoubled their efforts. As I drifted aimlessly through identikit days of lockdown and furlough, it was harder and harder to stay offline. Everybody else was online too, and it seemed like they were all having opinions about us. The government hosted a drawn out bungling of the Gender Recognition Act. This was ostensibly was about whether or not it would be appropriate to reduce the number of steps involved in obtaining a Gender Recognition Certificate, the document which acknowledges a trans person's gender in law. For some reason, the government thought it was appropriate to get the opinion of the whole country on this, meaning the hysteria around single-sex spaces was once again at a high. Anti-trans voices claimed that making the process easier would allow 'any man who believes or feels he's a woman'[1] to enter and cause harm – by which they insinuated that trans women are men, and dangerous ones at that. Trans women were once again in the firing line, and as usual the persistent news coverage set off microcosms of debate that made the social environment hostile for trans people in general.

Adhering to COVID regulations, I left the house exactly once a day. The fear and uncertainty of living through a pandemic was getting to me, and I found that walking out my front door, up through the parks and back down in a fifteen minute loop cleared my head-space enough to form a sort of firebreak between me and complete anxious breakdown. It wasn't quite joyful, but it was enough. I was taking what I could get. On one of these walks, I wandered past a forgotten hatchback that had been parked up on the pavement all year, gathering cobwebs and pigeon shit. A small pink sticker about the size of a business card had been slapped on to the rear driver's side door.

KEEP PRISONS SINGLE SEX, it said.

I couldn't shake the absurdity of it. I thought, *I am allowed out of my house for exactly one hour per day, and I am using part of that time to be transphobe'd by a car.* That, at least, made me laugh.

Around this time, a woman named Keira Bell was suing the Tavistock and Portman NHS trust for allowing her to medically transition. Now twenty-three, Bell contested that the centre should have challenged her more on her decision to transition to male, and should not have prescribed her puberty blockers at the age of sixteen. The judged ruled that puberty blockers could no longer be prescribed to under-sixteens without the authorisation of the courts. This meant that dozens of children awaiting treatment at the Tavistock's Gender Identity Development Service had their lives put on hold and some of their medical options withdrawn. Many families were devastated, and the media coverage kept coming.

KEIRA BELL LAWYER WARNS ON INTERNET
COVERAGE OF TRANSGENDER ISSUES[2]

OTHER COUNTRIES SHOULD LEARN FROM A
TRANSGENDER VERDICT IN ENGLAND[3]

KEIRA BELL CASE SHOWS WHY TRANSGENDER
RIGHTS DEBATE CAN'T BE PUT ON HOLD[4]

THE TIMES VIEW ON THE KEIRA BELL CASE:
FINE JUDGMENT[5]

WHY DID THE NHS LET ME CHANGE SEX?[6]

IT'S TIME FOR AN INQUIRY INTO THE DOCTORS
GIVING CHILDREN PUBERTY-BLOCKERS[7]

IN THE LIGHT OF THE KEIRA BELL CASE,
SCHOOLS NEED TO LOOK AT THEIR
APPROACH TO TRANSGENDER ISSUES[8]

And so on. This one case brought together every argument levied against trans people in the media and gave them the chance to point, unified, and go: *See? We were right all along.* This story was the proof; this was the definitive.

It is, of course, achingly sad that Keira Bell regrets her transition, and looks back on it with despair. The only correct approach in this situation is empathy. But other people's experiences, like my own and those of many people I know, are not the same. It isn't fair to suggest, as chatter around the case did, that trans men are pushed into transition because of society's restrictive image of womanhood and femininity. The media's coverage of the case again suggested that trans people – particularly young trans men, owing to the specifics of the case and the groups who were backing it – were brainwashed, and didn't know themselves. Transness was presented as something awful, to be shielded from. They were trying to spare people from it, from the spreading poison of what they term 'transgenderism', and its beguiling, brainwashing effects.

A confession: I do find transness beguiling. I was one thing, and now I am something else. Is that not a kind of magic? I am the person I always wanted to be. How can that be anything other than joyful?

I don't actually care whether or not I was born this way. I've seen myself as either a boy or a man for as long as I can remember, and so I assume that whatever it is that makes me transgender has been with me from the start, or close to it. Whether I came out of the womb like this, however, or whether I absorbed it as I was growing up is irrelevant. It's infantilising to be talked about in a way that, at best, implies that you're afflicted with something. This is by no means a view universally held among trans people but, to me, to plead for acceptance on the basis that I was 'born this way' misses the point. It suggests that I believe I'm in the wrong, that I would change it if I could. That if only I hadn't had the gross misfortune to be born trans I would gladly throw myself at the feet of cisnormativity and assimilate.

I would not change it if I could. I have no interest in being straight. Heterosexuality holds no wonders for me. And, increasingly, I have no desire to be cis either. It would make life easier, perhaps, but I've come to like it here, at the intersection of trans and gay. This is where the world feels most vivid to me.

Speaking to *The Guardian* around their phenomenally queer book *Paul Takes the Form of A Mortal Girl*, Andrea Lawlor told journalist Alex Needham, 'I feel that every good thing that has happened in my life has come from being queer.'[9] They were referring to their parenting situation, kinship and chosen family, but their delight in queerness struck a chord. I have found infinitely more joy in embracing my queerness and leaning in to it than I ever did trying to cover it up.

In Lawlor's novel it is 1993 and the protagonist, Paul, can shapeshift from one body to another. He can make his dick bigger or smaller, broaden his shoulders, change the shape of his face. He can change from a boy to a girl. It's easy to see why this appealed to me.

Paul can choose precisely how he is interpreted by the world. He can change his body to fit any situation, to blend in anywhere, and he uses this power to be relentlessly, deliciously queer. He works in a gay bookstore, goes to leather bars, and spends a week at the Michigan Womyn's Music Festival. He sleeps with boys when he is a boy and girls when he is a girl, and in the background of all this, always just slightly in shadow, is the ongoing AIDS crisis.

Reading as we slid towards summer in 2019, I felt a kind of giddy recognition. The trouble that I felt mired in was not the same as the epidemic that tore through so many gay and trans bodies from the early 1980s onwards, but I was reminded that queer joy has been marked by defiance. For people like us, uncomplicated happiness has not been the standard. It was embarrassing to have had to be prompted on what queer community organisers, LGBT elders and gay and trans people of colour had known for decades – that happiness *despite* is a radical act, and that we are liberated and elevated through each other. In spending so long outwardly denying my queerness, refusing to engage with it in any meaningful sort of way lest I be reduced and dismissed, I internally perpetuated the idea that I was lesser. I excluded myself from the community that could have been a source of support and meaning all along.

I didn't have the energy to do that to myself for the rest of my life, so I discarded it. The truth is, I'm delighted to be queer. It feels like getting away with something. It's as if I've found a secret door and slipped through it, and now I'm looking around like, *Does everyone know about this? Why isn't everybody queer when it feels like this?*

Of course, there are people who think I am actually getting away with something by being both trans and gay and being this delighted about it. Sometimes that makes it hard to hold on to. In late 2020, as the Bell v Tavistock case was heading to court and the government scrapped plans to make changes to the Gender Recognition Act, members of the LGB Alliance, a body that states its mission is 'to advance lesbian, gay and bisexual rights'[10] were kicking off that Mr Gay England had its first ever trans man finalist.

'Wakey wakey...gay boys. Did you sleep through the alarm? Did you decline those urgent calls from your lesbian sisters? Now it's YOUR turn to be gaslit as the trans project to destroy the very meaning of the word gay steps up a gear,' Alliance co-founder Malcolm Clark tweeted in October 2020.[11]

Naturally my first thought was 'grow up', but this is a major part of the LGB Alliance's rhetoric. Their organisation draws on the supposed narrative that gay trans people exist to the detriment of gay cis people.[12] [13] This was a well-worn topic from them in regards to trans women, and now they were ready to start on trans men.

I struggle to get my head around this kind of exclusion. If you don't want to sleep with me, then don't. That's fine. However, I find attempts to exclude both myself and any man who dates or has sex with me from the category of gay baffling.[14] [15] There's such a wide range of histories, attractions and viewpoints among gay men that it seems absurd to try and restrict the label to one set of experiences. Some gay men have only ever been attracted to other cis men, and some haven't. Some people who now consider themselves gay used to identify as bisexual. Some have been married to women. Do we really believe a man can only be gay if he's never encountered – and perhaps, dare I say it, enjoyed – a vagina even once in his entire life? Even Elton John has an ex-wife.

Gay trans men experience homophobia just the same as our cis counterparts. Nobody has ever asked me if I was born a boy before they called me a faggot, before they complained about poofs, before they told me they wished people still planted nail bombs in Soho so the gays wouldn't come around anymore. I've looked over my date's shoulder to check nobody was watching us kiss, let go of someone's hand on the walk home, stayed closeted at work and invented girlfriends to end an awkward line of questioning from a stranger. What good does it do any of us to pretend the fight for gay rights and acceptance doesn't apply to me?

When Chiyo Gomes was named a Mr Gay England finalist, he was in some small part representing people like me. When he became a target for transphobic attack, others stepped up – just as they always have for me. Writing for *Pink News*, journalist Vic Parsons reported that 'gay men themselves were swift to respond, and their condemnation of the LGB Alliance and its trans-exclusionary stance was brutal. "I'm a gay man and I say f**k you, you ignorant piece of s**t," was one succinct response.'[16]

It doesn't fix all the world's transphobia, but vocal allyship does provide a counterbalance. While it is tiring to need allies, to have to hope that someone will speak up for you in the face of transphobia, I've always been able to have faith in cis gay friends and romances. They remind me that I'm part of the same nebulous experience that they are. Chiyo himself was defiant, too, as he told *Attitude*:

> 'The people who take issue with me being visible in this space will tell you exactly how I am shaking things up. I am a trans man. I am also mixed-black African. I am not on hormones and I have no intention of getting any procedures done that may impact my [Wet Ass Pussy].'[17]

Alongside the interview, he was pictured in the November 2020 issue of the magazine emerging from a lake, chest reconstruction scars glistening on his torso. He was framed like a Hollywood leading man. He was not presented as a novelty or as an interloper, but as deserving of his place in the competition. In this picture, Chiyo's body was celebrated the same way that all the other finalists' bodies were. It went against what the reigning sentiment in the media had been for so many months – that transition was traumatic, upsetting, something to be discouraged as far as possible, and that trans bodies were damaged or abnormal.

I reject the oft-spouted idea from anti-trans voices that transmasculine bodies are mutilated.[18] [19] [20] [21] I dreamt of this body, and I celebrate it, even if it hasn't turned out exactly to my specifications. Trans bodies are often portrayed as sites of horror, trauma and dysphoria, or as examples of medical or scientific overreach. I prefer to think of trans bodies as sources of love and desire. We have partners, we date, we are intimate. I still feel gender euphoria when I place my palm flat in the centre of my chest, or when I catch the angle of my jaw in the mirror. There remains a femininity to my physicality that I wouldn't trade, and I have been called both slinky and sprite-like by other men. This body feels ethereal. I had to pass through another realm to get it.

Conclusion
On Joy

So where do we land? I have been trying to think of an elegant way to conclude this. But maybe it's fitting to be inconclusive. Like myself, happiness is a shapeshifter.

Going into this book, I wasn't sure how I'd talk about transmasculine joy. I made a provisional list of books by and about trans men, and that was about as far as I got. It was the tail end of 2020, my personal life was once again an absolute shambles, and now I had a book to write. About joy. Even though I had a much better grasp on it by this point than I had when I initially thought about pursuing a happier, more balanced narrative at the close of the original Appendix, it was still near-impossible to quantify.

As I began this project, the second coming of The Appendix, there were still people in my life I hadn't told I was trans. Earlier in the book, I asked how you broach a subject like that multiple years into a friendship. In my case the answer was, apparently, that you wait for a Hollywood celebrity to come out as transmasculine, and then you write about him.

When Elliot Page publicly shared the news of his transition at the beginning of December 2020, I was delighted. For years, I'd felt an unexplainable kinship with him. When I was a tomboy teen, he was playing them in *Juno* and *Whip It* and, ironically, I used to point to his public persona as proof that not all boyish girls were gay or trans. I would use it as evidence that I, too, was not necessarily gay or trans. This was funny when I transitioned and funnier still when Elliot came out as gay in 2014, and when he shared news of his transition with the world it felt to me like some final piece clicking in to place. As if in some strange way he and I had been on this trip together.

The mood in my house that night was celebratory. We laughed about the fact that he had chosen one of what the trans community lovingly call The Names – Alex, Oliver, Elliot, Aiden, Jayden, Brayden, Kaden, and the various spellings thereof, which have been adopted so widely by trans men that they've become something of a cliché.

'I feel like I should congratulate you,' my friend said of Elliot joining our ranks.

'Thank you,' I said. 'It's a big day for us.'

I wrote a piece for *Dazed* trying to capture my happiness at Elliot's announcement, knowing that once it was published there would be no going back. When the piece went live, I would be publicly trans. I was jittery. It was exciting.

After the article went up, I posted a small Twitter thread.

'That *Dazed* piece is a big deal for me lads. I transitioned nearly a decade ago, but I've never written about it. When I moved to London I kept it quiet for about 4.5 years. Only told romantic partners and a few close friends.

'I fully intended to keep it that way. It was one of the reasons I moved here in the first place. But it made me so, so ill. And any time another trans person died, or there was a snarky headline, I couldn't talk about it.

'It's only in the last 2 years or so I've decided people can take me exactly as I am, or they can fuck off. And mostly I've stuck to that. But it's not a good time to be trans, so in writing I've stayed half in and half out.'

I wrapped up with a declaration, something I was only just coming to fully understand:

'Elliot's announcement was important. More often than not, it makes a difference to not be standing alone. It made a difference to me.'

Then I waited for the serotonin boost of that little blue number popping up on my notifications tab. It started climbing.

The response from my friends was overwhelmingly positive. I should have known it would be, and yet somehow I hadn't accounted for this. People called me brave, which was kind but untrue, and friends shared the article and told me they were proud of me, that I was loved.

I hadn't anticipated the strength I felt. Feel. The yoga videos I'd taken to watching sporadically in lockdown were always telling me to ground down through my feet, and suddenly I felt like I was doing it all the time. I'd created space in my body.

I'm not sure if this was what you'd call joy. Mostly, what it felt like was relief. I'd already agreed to write this book when the Elliot Page article was commissioned, and at the time I was a little apprehensive. For years I'd been going back and forth on whether I wanted to write about my experience of being trans, worried that if I did it I would want to take it back. But once the *Dazed* piece was published and my real self was out there, I was glad. Being trans stopped feeling like something I needed to cover up or suppress, and instead became something worth embracing. I had meant what I said in my tweet, that people could take me as I am or fuck off, and acknowledging that both to myself and the general public was freeing.

This was the kind of energy I was trying to bring to this book. I didn't always manage it, as I excavated my past experiences with transphobia and tried to put them into something resembling a coherent narrative, but now at the end of the process the feeling is back.

When I set out to collate The Appendix mark one in 2019, what I was looking for was a reprieve from the onslaught. The idea that I could somehow put a stopper in transphobia was misguided, but looking back the project achieved what it was supposed to on a personal level. The original Appendix spawned this Appendix, and this Appendix has allowed me to consider joy in all its complexity, to sit with my transness and think about my relationship to it. It has given me the impetus, finally, to set aside shame. To refuse to carry that which does not belong to me.

What a luxury.

It's important to note again here, at the close, that the circumstances which have allowed me to write this book are also the factors that limit its perspective. I am white, I am male 'passing', and I have a stable job and a safe home life. Mine is not the key trans experience, or the worst, or the most broadly applicable. It is only mine. It matters only when taken as part of a larger whole, one of many perspectives on what it is like to be trans in this country, at this moment. These are only my thoughts, my experiences, on joy.

In recent years, there's been an increase in the number of books by trans authors being published. Or maybe I'm just paying more attention now. In 2021, Torrey Peters' novel *Detransition, Baby* saw her become the first trans woman to be longlisted for the Women's Prize for Fiction, her inclusion made possible by the work of Akwaeke Emezi, who challenged the prize over their policies in 2020 after their novel *Freshwater* was longlisted despite the fact that Emezi is nonbinary.[1]

Alongside Peters and Emezi – as well writers such as Travis Alabanza, Shon Faye, Shola von Reinhold and Paris Lees, to name a few in the UK specifically – contemporary trans canon also includes writing by many transmasculine people, who are producing work not only on gender, masculinity and transness, but also climate change, community, race, tradition, love, sex, healing, magic – and, yes, joy. The joy of self-actualisation, of falling in love, finding community, and shrugging off shame. This is the literary tradition that I am privileged to be entering into. That I hope my voice contributes something valuable to.

Given that recent years have also seen a proliferation of titles by gender critical authors, it remains to be seen whether the platforming of trans writers is a genuine progression or the cynical exploitation of a trend from the perspective of publishers. Meaningful change takes time and work. But regardless of the motivations of the wider publishing industry, trans stories are out there. They are finding readers and providing an alternate narrative to the doom and gloom that so often dominates the stories told about us from the outside. Because they are still being told.

In the time it took me to conceive of and write this book, nearly 300 news stories about trans people were published in mainstream British papers. I know this because I needed a few sources here and there, some context, so I looked them up. I went to the news sites and did a search all for the category 'transgender', picked out what I needed and counted up the total. 280 news stories, between September 2020 and March 2021.

My flatmates came home in the middle of this endeavour, while I was sitting on the sofa with my laptop propped up against my knees.

'Isn't that the exact thing that set you off the first time?' they asked.

'No,' I said.

Yes, I thought. They had a point. As usual, my friends are the keepers of my sanity. I got in, did the job, and got out, like a well-executed bank heist. When I closed the computer, I didn't feel bothered at all. I believe that's what they call progress.

So political parties are still debating our rights, books by transphobes are coming out from major presses, and not long ago, somewhere in the depths of the internet, a man I had never heard of brought my profile to the attention of anti-trans campaigners. I just muted him and moved on. It was easier than it used to be. The foundations for my trans joy are more stable now.

Gender euphoria is not as clear cut as it was when I was a kid. Back then, it was enough just to be seen as a boy. Now it comes from being welcomed into a group of men, or standing at the back of a gig with a plastic pint in my hand. It comes in conversation with other queer people and in communion with other queer bodies. I feel it when I glance at myself in the mirror and notice that, finally, the person that I am fits just right. It's there when I am drinking red wine and dancing to Pulp in my beloved silver Doc Martens, when I am walking down the street to meet my friends, when I am trying to stay awake on the night tube home. Gender euphoria and trans joy now are just products of my daily life, no longer distinct experiences but a sustained contentment that I couldn't access when I was trying to hold transness at arm's length. I don't worry anymore about being 'too' anything. Who has the energy for that?

I keep coming back to that line in the film. *So you're a boy. Now what?*

Now this. Now life.

References

Introduction:
A Terrible Idea That Will Make You Sick

1. "Thanks to Hornsey & Wood Green Labour Party for passing this motion in support of women's rights, trans rights and the right to respectful debate. Thank you to the 4 branches who all tabled it. This is an excellent way forward. We hope others will do the same." @Womans_Place_UK. *Twitter*, 24 October 2019, 12:34PM, https://twitter.com/Womans_Place_UK/status/1187331576113352705/photo/1. Accessed 13 July 2021.
2. "EXCLUSIVE: Mermaids' research into newspaper coverage on trans issues." Mermaids Press, Mermaids, 18 November 2019, mermaidsuk.org.uk/news/exclusive-mermaids-research-into-newspaper-coverage-on-trans-issues/. Accessed 13 July 2021.

Chapter 2:
Won't Somebody *Please* Think of the Children?

1. Howard Cunnell, Fathers and Sons. Picador, 2017. p128.
2. "Trans children allowed to express identity 'have good mental health'". Amanda Holpuch, *The Guardian*, 26 February 2016. www.theguardian.com/society/2016/feb/26/crucial-study-transgender-children-mental-health-family-support. Accessed 13 July 2021.

3. "Affirmative care may elicit the best mental health outcomes in transgender youths." *The Association for Child and Adolescent Mental Health*, 25 August 2020. www.acamh.org/research-digest/affirmative-care/. Accessed 13 July 2021.

4. "Impacts of Strong Parental Support for Trans Youth." *Trans PULSE*, 2 October 2012. transpulseproject.ca/wp-content/uploads/2012/10/Impacts-of-Strong-Parental-Support-for-Trans-Youth-vFINAL.pdf. Accessed 13 July 2021.

5. Ryan, Caitlin, et al. (2010). "Family acceptance in adolescence and the health of LGBT young adults." *Journal of Child and Adolescent Psychiatric Nursing*, Vol. 23, No. 4, doi.org/10.1111/j.1744-6171.2010.00246.x

6. Linehan, creator of popular sitcoms including Father Ted and Black Books, had his Twitter account permanently suspended in June 2020 after 'repeated violations of [Twitter's] rules against hateful conduct and platform manipulation' due to his regular 'gender critical' commentary. www.theguardian.com/culture/2020/jun/27/twitter-closes-graham-linehan-account-after-trans-comment. Accessed 13 July 2021.

7. Webb tweeted in December 2018, 'This won't make me popular in certain quarters but fuck it – I'm with Janice and I don't say it often enough. Also @boodleoops also @bindelj I've talked to some really nice trans people here & they have my solidarity if they want it. But Mermaids sucks.' The tweet has since been deleted but a screenshot can be found on Pink News: www.pinknews.co.uk/2020/04/13/robert-webb-bigot-trans-charity-mermaids-sucks-transphobia-gender-critical-peep-show-janice-turner/. Accessed 13 July 2021.
He later tweeted 'I'm a gender-critical feminist.' twitter.com/arobertwebb/status/1076525911250530304. Accessed 13 July 2021.

8. "#EndConversionTherapy." LGB Alliance, lgballiance.org.uk/endconversiontherapy/. Accessed 13 July 2021.

9. "It feels like conversion therapy for gay children, say clinicians." Lucy Bannerman, *The Times*, 8 April 2019. www.

thetimes.co.uk/article/it-feels-like-conversion-therapy-for-gay-children-say-clinicians-pvsckdvq2. Accessed 13 July 2021.

10. "Robert Webb criticised for attacking trans kids charity Mermaids." Josh Jackman, *Pink News*, 24 December 2018. www.pinknews.co.uk/2018/12/24/robert-webb-trans-kids-mermaids/. Accessed 15 July 2021.

11. "The toys and clothing question." mermaids_author, Mermaids, 20 July 2020. mermaidsuk.org.uk/news/the-toys-and-clothing-question/. Accessed 13 July 2021.

12. "Puberty blockers and consent to treatment: an analysis of the High Court's ruling." Community Care, 11 December 2020. www.communitycare.co.uk/2020/12/11/puberty-block-ers-consent-treatment-analysis-high-courts-ruling/. Accessed 13 July 2021.

Chapter 3:
The Appendix

1. "Section 28: What was it and how did it affect LGBT+ people?" Harvey Day, *BBC Three*, 1 November 2019. www.bbc.co.uk/bbcthree/article/cacc0b40-c3a4-473b-86cc-11863c0b3f30. Accessed 13 July 2021.

2. Chastagner, Claude. (1999). "The Parents' Music Resource Center: From Information to Censorship." *Popular Music*, Vol. 18, No. 2, pp. 179-192. www.jstor.org/stable/853600. Accessed 13 July 2021.

3. "Calls to end transgender 'experiment on children'." Lucy Bannerman, *The Times*, 8 April 2019. www.thetimes.co.uk/article/calls-to-end-transgender-experiment-on-children-k792rfj7d. Accessed 13 July 2021.

4. "Families 'exploited by gender lobby groups pushing for treat-ment'." Lucy Bannerman, *The Times*, 8 April 2019. www.thetimes.co.uk/article/families-exploited-by-gender-lobby-groups-push-ing-for-treatment-5fddvml8r. Accessed 13 July 2021.

5. "Doubts over evidence for using drugs on the young." Professor Carl Heneghan, *The Times*, 8 April 2019. www.thetimes. co.uk/article/doubts-over-evidence-for-using-drugs-on-the-young-2vk26hrvx. Accessed 13 July 2021.

6. "It feels like conversion therapy for gay children, say clinicians." Lucy Bannerman, *The Times*, 8 April 2019. www. thetimes.co.uk/article/it-feels-like-conversion-therapy-for-gay-children-say-clinicians-pvsckdvq2. Accessed 13 July 2021.

7. mermaidsuk.org.uk/parents/. Accessed 13 July 2021.

8. "Mother who called trans woman 'he' on Twitter is CLEARED of wrongdoing after appealing against conviction." George Odling, *The Daily Mail*, 11 December 2020. www.dailymail.co.uk/news/article-9041725/Mum-called-trans-woman-Twitter-CLEARED-wrongdoing.html. Accessed 13 July 2021.

9. "Women slam Tampax over tweet celebrating the 'diversity of all people who bleed' amid calls for boycott." Jack Newman, 25 October 2020. www.dailymail.co.uk/news/article-8877425/Tampax-slammed-tweet-celebrating-diversity-people-bleed-amid-calls-boycott.html. Accessed 13 July 2021.

10. "Lesbians facing 'extinction' as transgenderism becomes pervasive, campaigners warn." Camilla Tominey, *The Telegraph*, 25 December 2020. www.telegraph.co.uk/news/2020/12/25/lesbians-facing-extinction-transgenderism-becomes-pervasive/. Accessed 13 July 2021.

11. "'I'm not transphobic and I never have been,' says Father Ted's Graham Linehan." Emily Hourican, *The Irish Independent*, 7 April 2019. www.independent.ie/irish-news/im-not-transphobic-and-i-never-have-been-says-father-teds-graham-linehan-37990105.html. Accessed 13 July 2021.

12. "John Boyne: Why I support trans rights but reflect the word 'cis'." John Boyne, *The Irish Times*, 13 April 2019. www.irishtimes.com/culture/books/john-boyne-why-i-support-trans-rights-but-reject-the-word-cis-1.3843005. Accessed 13 July 2021.

13. Ibid.
14. "Objections to 'Cis'." *Not the News in Briefs*, 16 July 2020. notthenewsinbriefs.wordpress.com/2020/07/16/objections-to-cis/. Accessed 13 July 2021.
15. "Am I cisgender?" boodleoops, *Medium*, 17 June 2020. medium.com/@rebeccarc/am-i-cisgender-d337512176d. Accessed 13 July 2021.
16. @Docstockk, Kathleen Stock, *Twitter*. twitter.com/Docstockk/status/1411586474319953920. Accessed 13 July 2021.
17. "The author John Boyne is wrong to pander to trans activists." Kim Thomas, *The Spectator*, 18 April 2019. www.spectator.co.uk/article/the-author-john-boyne-is-wrong-to-pander-to-trans-activists. Accessed 13 July 2021.
18. "John Boyne is a man, not a 'cis' man." Ella Whelan, *Spiked*, 25 April 2019. www.spiked-online.com/2019/04/25/john-boyne-is-a-man-not-a-cis-man/. Accessed 13 July 2021.
19. "SNP ministers urge caution over sex 'definition change'." Gina Davidson, *The Scotsman*, 24 April 2019. www.pressreader.com/uk/the-scotsman/20190424/281496457690642. Accessed 13 July 2021.

Chapter 4:
Not 'Born This Way'

1. "Explainer: J. K. Rowling and trans women in single-sex spaces: what's the furore?" Amber Milne, Rachel Savage, *Reuters*, 11 June 2020. www.reuters.com/article/us-britain-lgbt-rowling-explainer-trfn-idUSKBN23I3AI. Accessed 13 July 2021.
2. "Keira Bell lawyer warns on internet coverage of transgender issues." Jamie Doward, *The Guardian*, 6 December 2020. www.theguardian.com/uk-news/2020/dec/06/keira-bell-lawyer-warns-on-internet-coverage-of-transgender-issues. Accessed 13 July 2021.

3. "Other countries should learn from a transgender verdict in England." *The Economist*, 10 December 2020. www.economist. com/leaders/2020/12/12/other-countries-should-learn-from-a-transgender-verdict-in-england. Accessed 13 July 2021.

4. "Keira Bell case shows why transgender rights debate can't be put on hold." Shona Craven, *The National*, 4 December 2020. www.thenational.scot/news/18919508.shona-craven-mens-rants-must-not-drown-child-protection-fears/. Accessed 13 July 2021.

5. "The Times view on the Keira Bell case: Fine Judgement." *The Times*, 2 December 2020. www.thetimes.co.uk/article/the-times-view-on-the-keira-bell-case-fine-judgment-8v5vvwnwm. Accessed 13 July 2021.

6. "Why did the NHS let me change sex? Star witness in court battle against clinic that fast-tracked her gender swap aged 16 reveals what happened when she made a cry for help." Sue Reid, *The Daily Mail*, 24 January 2020. www.dailymail.co.uk/news/article-7926675/Witness-court-battle-against-gender-clinic-reveals-happened-cry-help.html. Accessed 13 July 2021.

7. "It's time for an inquiry into the doctors giving children puberty-blockers." James Kirkup, *The Telegraph*, 2 December 2020. www.telegraph.co.uk/news/2020/12/02/time-inquiry-doctors-giving-children-puberty-blockers/. Accessed 13 July 2021.

8. "In light of the Keira Bell case, schools need to look at their approach to transgender issues." NewsDesk, *ExBulletin*, 4 December 2020. exbulletin.com/world/596340/. Accessed 13 July 2021.

9. "Andrea Lawlor: 'I feel that every good thing in my life has come from being queer'." Alex Needham, *The Guardian*, 5 April 2019. www.theguardian.com/books/2019/apr/05/andrea-lawlor-dont-want-to-be-representative-of-a-type. Accessed 13 July 2021.

10. "Our Mission." LGB Alliance. lgballiance.org.uk/about/. Accessed 13 July 2021.

11. "1./ Wakey wakey...gay boys. Did you sleep through the alarm? Did you decline those urgent calls from your lesbian sisters? Now it's YOUR turn to be gaslit as the trans project to destroy the very meaning of the word gay steps up a gear." @TwisterFilm, Malcolm Clark, *Twitter*, 10 October 2020, 3:32PM. twitter.com/TwisterFilm/status/1314936969986703360. Accessed 13 July 2021.

12. A link on the LGB Alliance's Myths page (lgballiance.org.uk/myths/) leads to the following article in The Times, which suggests that people are transitioning as a result of homophobia. ("It feels like conversion therapy for gay children, say clinicians." Lucy Bannerman, *The Times*, 8 April 2019. www.thetimes.co.uk/article/it-feels-like-conversion-therapy-for-gay-children-say-clinicians-pvsckdvq2. Accessed 13 July 2021.)

13. Under a different heading on the same webpage, the LGB Alliance link to an article on Fair Play for Women, which states that 'The denial of biological sex also erases homosexuality, as as same-sex attraction is meaningless without the distinction between the sexes. Many activists now define homosexuality as attraction to the "same gender identity" rather than the same sex. This view is at odds with the scientific understanding of human sexuality.' ("Sex is binary: Scientists speak up for the empirical reality of biological sex." Fair Play For Women, 14 February 2020. fairplayforwomen.com/scientistsspeak/. Accessed 13 July 2021.)
"The LGB Alliance is not transphobic – we are just trying to protect ourselves." Ceri Black, *The Irish Independent*, 10 November 2020. www.independent.ie/opinion/comment/the-lgb-alliance-is-not-transphobic-we-are-just-trying-to-protect-ourselves-39727908.html. Accessed 13 July 2021.

14. "The Gay Spot – Are gay men getting lost in the gender identity debate?" Bev Jackson & Kate Harris, *Eventbrite*, 26 November 2020. www.eventbrite.co.uk/e/the-gay-spot-are-gay-men-getting-lost-in-the-gender-identity-debate-tickets-129023818715. Accessed 13 July 2021.

15. "Register now for our fabulous webinar Thu 26 Nov at 1900! This time it's all about men! "The Gay Spot – are gay men getting lost in the gender identity debate?" #SexNotGender." LGB Alliance, *Twitter*, 21 November 2020, 10:36AM. twitter.com/alliancelgb/status/1330097831772905473. Accessed 13 July 2021.

16. "Mr Gay England's first trans finalist Chiyo Gomes targeted by vile LGB Alliance attack. Fortunately, nobody was having any of it." Vic Parsons, *Pink News*, 13 October 2020. www.pinknews.co.uk/2020/10/13/chiyo-gomes-mr-gay-england-finalist-attacked-lgb-alliance/. Accessed 13 July 2021.

17. "Mr Gay England's first trans finalist Chiyo Gomes: 'TERFs genuinely want to destroy the trans existence." *Attitude*, 7 October 2020. attitude.co.uk/article/mr-gay-englands-first-trans-finalist-chiyo-gomes-terfs-genuinely-want-to-destroy-the-trans-existence-1/23833/. Accessed 13 July 2021.

18. One tweet said: "She's a spicey straight with a mutilated body. Nothing progressive about any of this. The worst thing is, more girls will think this is a good idea. Look at my work on the medical aspect of this. Trans people need mental health, not cosmetic surgery"

19. Another tweet: "Those men aren't gay. You're confusing gay men with heterosexual fetishists and the ever increasing number of mutilated, heterosexual women on T."

20. Chiyo's response to above tweets:
    "They say:
    MUTILATED WOMAN
    COSPLAYING THAT GUY FROM THE UMBRELLA ACADEMY
    DRUGGED UP JOHNNY DEPP
    CONFUSED STRAIGHT GIRL
    CO-OPTING GAY CULTURE
    and I smile. Mmmmmm don't you just love the tears of a bigot? 😊

Here's me giving zero fucks at #LondonTransPride last week💚" @PrinxChiyo, Chiyo Gomes, *Twitter*, 16 September 2020, 4:16PM. twitter.com/prinxchiyo/status/1306250603644047360. Accessed 13 July 2021.

21. "Transgender man's mastectomy surgery dubbed 'mutilation'." Jared Lawthom, *BBC News*, 19 July 2019. www.bbc.co.uk/news/uk-wales-48990119. Accessed 13 July 2021.

Conclusion:
On Joy

1. "Popping back in to kick a hornet's nest ☺ My novels will notbe submitted for the Women's Prize. Their origin story is that men were excluding them w/the Booker, so when FRESHWATER was longlisted, I hoped it was a sign that they gave thought to who *they* were excluding." @azemezi, Akwaeke Emezi, *Twitter*, 5 October 2020, 7:30AM. twitter.com/azemezi/status/1313003554018332673. Accessed 13 July 2021.

Acknowledgements

Thank you to Laura Jones and Heather McDaid at 404 Ink for publishing this book, for their editorial expertise, and general hand-holding. Thanks also to Luke Bird for immortalising my beloved silver Docs in such a joyful cover design.

I was going to be reserved here, but after 15,000 words of overshare, what's a little more?

My life would never have been stable enough for me to write this book were it not for the family I chose. Hannah Webb and Raquel Palmeira, I love and am grateful for you every day. Our home together has been the luckiest break of my adult life.

Thank you to Jenn Thompson and Ellis for their support in life, writing, and queerness, and for always making me feel cool. Thank you to Jake Hawkes, Jamie Muir and Ali Shutler for their friendship and support despite the fact that I am objectively terrible. Particular thanks to Jake for always being on hand for a reality check.

This book is dedicated to my parents, with all the love and gratitude that I possess. Cheers for the sense of humour.

Finally, thank you to everyone who bought this book because they recognised me off a dating app that shall remain nameless. That's queer solidarity, baby.

About the Author

Liam Konemann is a queer Australian writer based in London. In 2019/20 he participated in Spread the Word's London Writers Awards scheme, and placed second for fiction in Streetcake Magazine's Experimental Writing Prize. He writes music journalism, fiction and poetry with a focus on queerness and masculinity. His debut novel will be published by 404 Ink in 2022.

Twitter: @LiamKonemann

About the Inklings series

This book is part of 404 Ink's Inkling series which presents big ideas in pocket-sized books.

They are all available at 404ink.com/shop.

If you enjoyed this book, you may also enjoy these titles in the series:

The New University: Local Solutions to a Global Crisis – James Coe

The New University considers the enormous challenge of reimagining how our public realm can function in a post-COVID landscape, and the institutions that form an indelible part of our civic life. Coe reimagines the University as a more civic and personal institution, believing we can get there through realigning our research to communal benefit.

Blind Spot: Exploring and Educating on Blindness – Maud Rowell

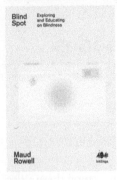

When it comes to blindness, people can often have many questions and few answers. In *Blind Spot*, Maud educates about the realities of living with sight loss, offering the knowledge they need to become better, more tolerant members of diverse communities.

No Man's Land: Living Between Two Cultures – Anne East

In *No Man's Land*, Anne explores this chasm in more detail, how it is to feel one thing and yet be perceived as another. What are the emotions that people feel in this limbo? Why is culture so important? And how does it feel to experience that cultural no man's land? A book on acceptance and shining a light on the cultural vacuum that exists for many, this is a must read from a voice rarely heard.